AF449057

BRILLIANT ANIMALS OF EVERY COLOR

-YELLOW-

CATHLEEN ROACH AND LUCAS DANIEL

FOR UNCLE LAWRENCE –
THE ORIGINAL "PARROT MAN".
YOU ARE ONE OF THE MANY
REASONS OUR LOVE OF ANIMALS
IS SO HUGE. THANK YOU!

HOW TO USE THIS BOOK:
NAME OF CREATURE
AMERICAN ALLIGATOR
FAMILY IT BELONGS TO
-REPTILE-
FACTS ABOUT SIZE, LOCATION, DIET, AND LIFESPAN
LENGTH : 12 - 17 FEET
WEIGHT: 500 - 2000 POUNDS
LIFESPAN : 70 YEARS
LOCATED : SOUTHEAST NORTH AMERICA
DIET : FISH, TURTLES, BIRDS, AND MAMMALS

CANNOT LIVE IN SALT WATER DUE TO THE INABILITY TO GET RID OF THE HIGH SALT CONTENT

RAINBOW FACTS ARE A FUN BONUS!

BODY FACTS

CAN MOVE SURPRISINGLY FAST – GOING UP TO 20 MPH IN THE WATER

WORLD MAP

ARCTIC OCEAN
NORTH AMERICA
EUROPE
ATLANTIC OCEAN
AFRICA
PACIFIC OCEAN
SOUTH AMERICA
ATLANTIC OCEAN
N
W
E
S
ANTARCTIC OCEAN
ANTARCTICA

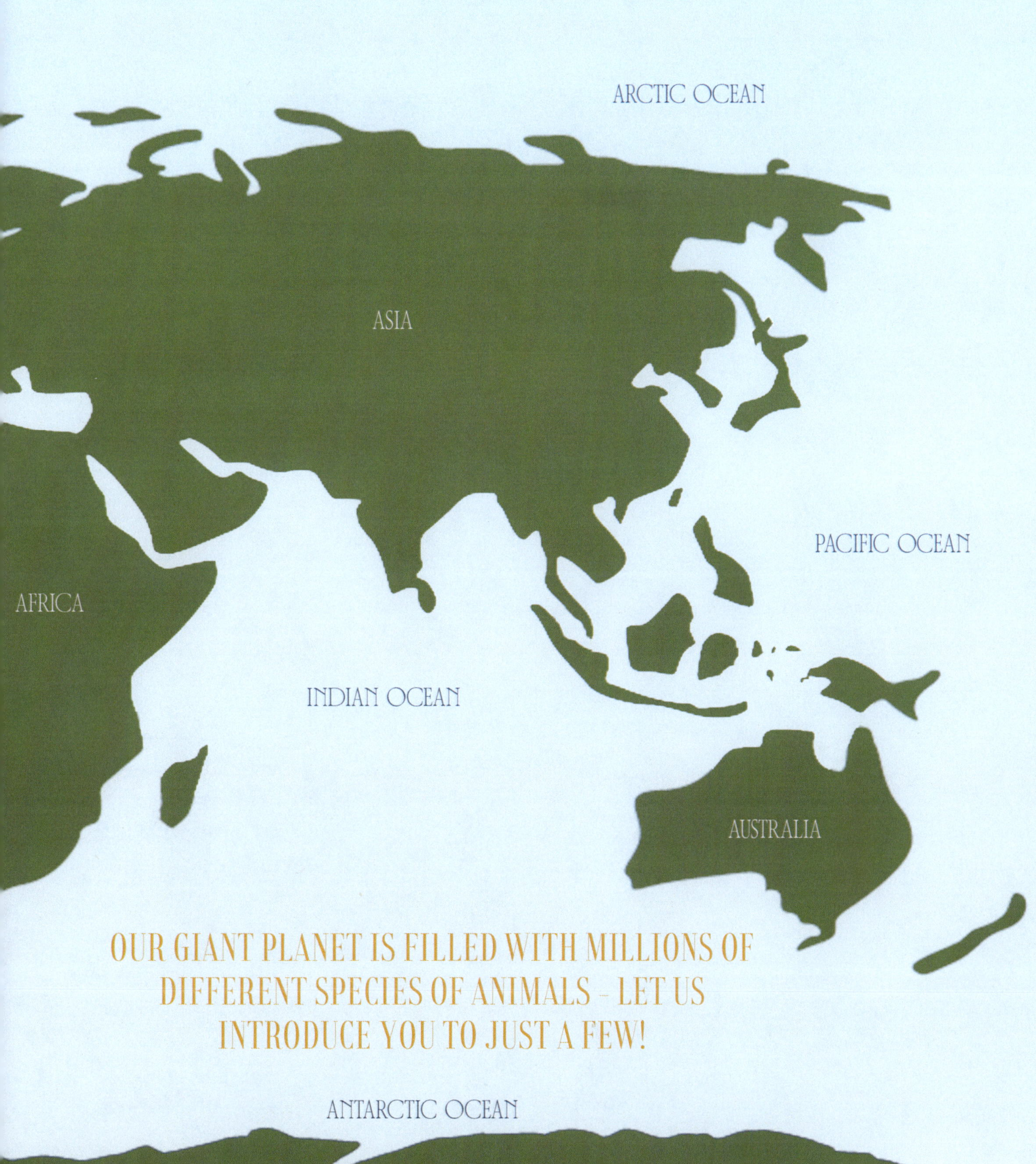

OUR GIANT PLANET IS FILLED WITH MILLIONS OF DIFFERENT SPECIES OF ANIMALS – LET US INTRODUCE YOU TO JUST A FEW!

HABITATS

BE ON THE LOOKOUT FOR THESE SYMBOLS LOCATED ON EACH PAGE. THEY WILL HELP YOU LEARN ABOUT WHERE EACH CREATURE IS FOUND IN OUR FANTASTIC WORLD!

COLD AND ICY
ENVIROMENT

RIVERS, LAKES,
AND PONDS

HUGE BODY OF
SALT WATER

DRY AND SANDY
ENVIROMENT

OPEN FIELDS OF
GRASS OR WHEAT

DENSE FOREST WITH
INTENSE RAINFALL

FILLED WITH TREES
AND UNDERGROWTH

HIGH ELEVATION
WITH RUGGED TERRAIN

LARGE TREELESS AREA
WITH HEAVY SNOWFALL

ENDANGERED SCALE

ON EACH PAGE YOU WILL FIND THIS SYMBOL.

IT REPRESENTS THE RANGE, OR AMOUNT
OF THREAT EACH ANIMAL HAS FOR EXTINCTION.
THIS SCALE IS CONSANTLY CHANGING, WHICH
IS WHY IT IS CRITICAL THAT WE DO
ALL WE CAN TO HELP THE ENVIROMENT.

YOU CAN HELP BY RECYCLING, NOT LITTERING, USING
LESS PLASTIC, AND PLANTING MORE TREES!

ALWAYS TALK TO YOUR PARENTS FIRST, AND
TOGETHER WE CAN MAKE OUR WONDERFUL
PLANET A BETTER PLACE FOR EVERYONE!

SIZE REFERENCE

BULLET ANT - 60 MILLIGRAMS 
(SMALLEST CREATURE IN OUR SERIES)

DEATHSTALKER SCORPION - 1 GRAM
(ROUGHLY 16 ANTS)

GREATER BULLDOG BAT - 1 OUNCE
(ROUGHLY 28 SCORPIONS)

LONG- WATTLED
UMBRELLABIRD - 1 POUND
(ROUGHLY 16 BATS)

BLUE WHALE - 350,000 POUNDS
(ROUGHLY 350,000 UMBRELLABIRDS)

(LARGEST CREATURE IN OUR SERIES)

CONVERSIONS

1000 MILLIGRAMS = 1 GRAM

28 GRAMS = 1 OUNCE

16 OUNCES = 1 POUND

LENGTH

2 1/2 CENTIMETERS = 1 INCH

12 INCHES = 1 FOOT

THAT MEANS ROUGHLY
2,646,000,000 BULLET ANTS
EQUAL 1 BLUE WHALE!

ENDANGERED SCALE
ONLY THE MALES
HAVE THE
MANE AROUND
THE FACE

INCREDIBLY SOCIAL
CATS LIVING IN LARGE
GROUPS CALLED PRIDES

AFRICAN LION

-MAMMAL-

LENGTH : 8 – 10 FEET

WEIGHT : 200 – 800 POUNDS

LIFESPAN : 16 YEARS

LOCATED : AFRICA

DIET : BUFFALO, ZEBRAS
SMALL ANTELOPE, AND GAZELLES

THEY HAVE FIVE EYES –
TWO ARE LARGE AND ON THE SIDES
AND THE EXTRA THREE ARE IN
THE TOP OF THEIR HEAD
ENDANGERED SCALE
LARGEST WASP IN
THE WORLD

ASIAN GIANT HORNET

-INSECT-

LENGTH : 2 INCHES

WEIGHT : 1 OUNCE

LIFESPAN : 3 -5 MONTHS

LOCATED : ASIA

DIET : OTHER INSECTS, BEETLES, AND DEAD ANIMALS

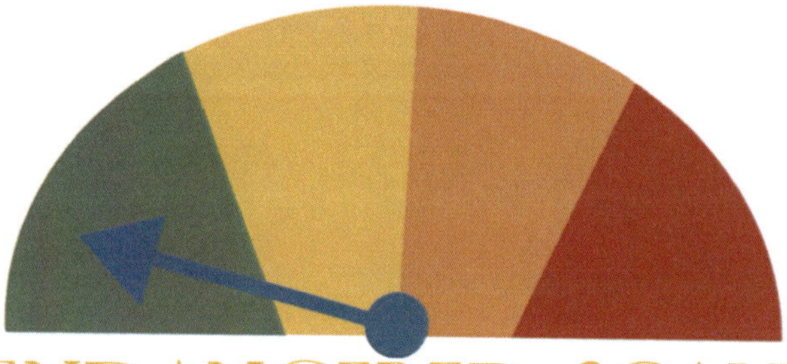

9 INCH WINGSPAN

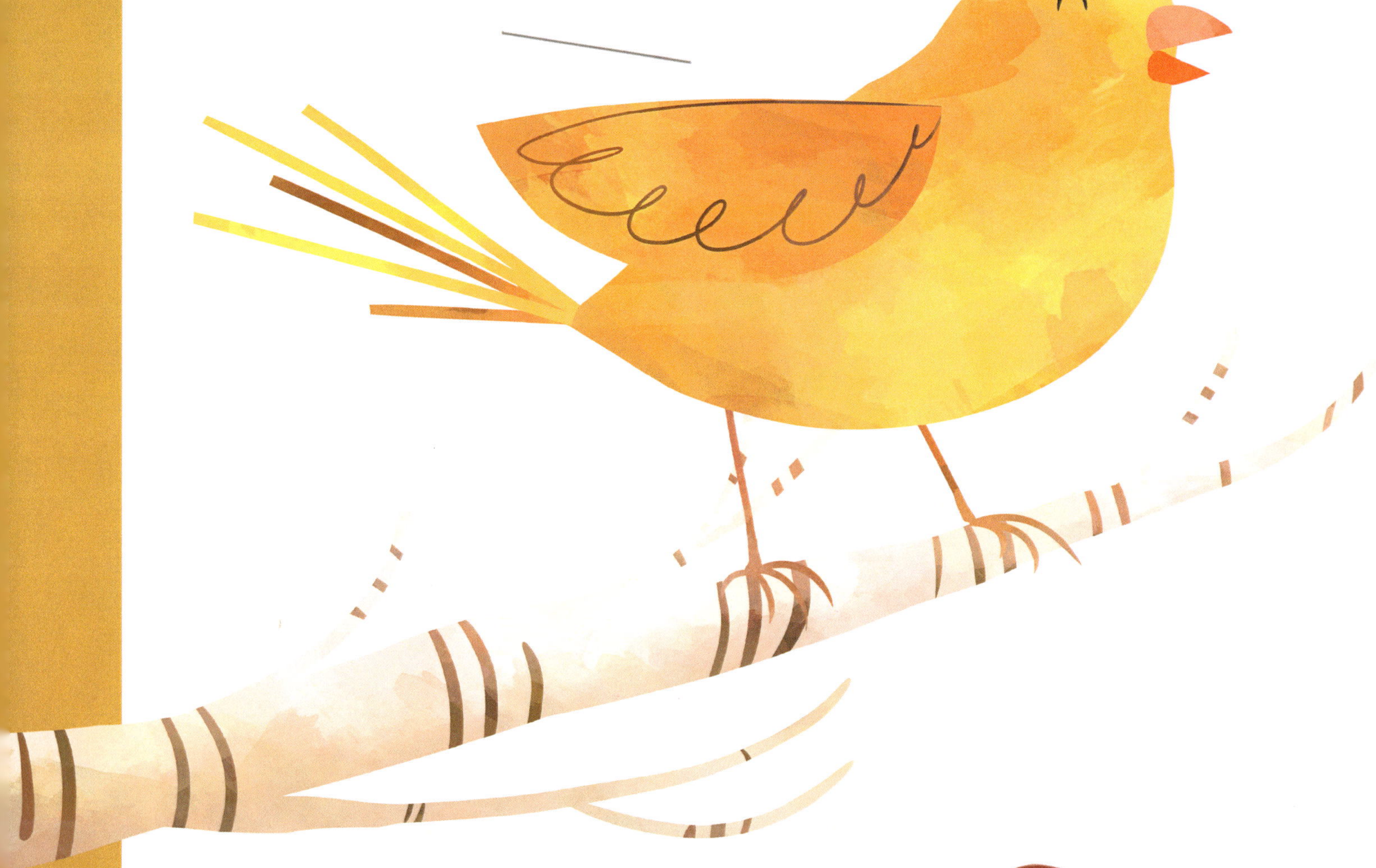

COMMON HOUSEHOLD PET
THAT IS KNOWN FOR ITS
BEAUTIFUL SINGING VOICE

CANARY

-BIRD-

LENGTH : 6 INCHES

WEIGHT : 20 GRAMS

LIFESPAN : 15 YEARS

LOCATED : CANARY ISLANDS

DIET : SEEDS AND GRAINS

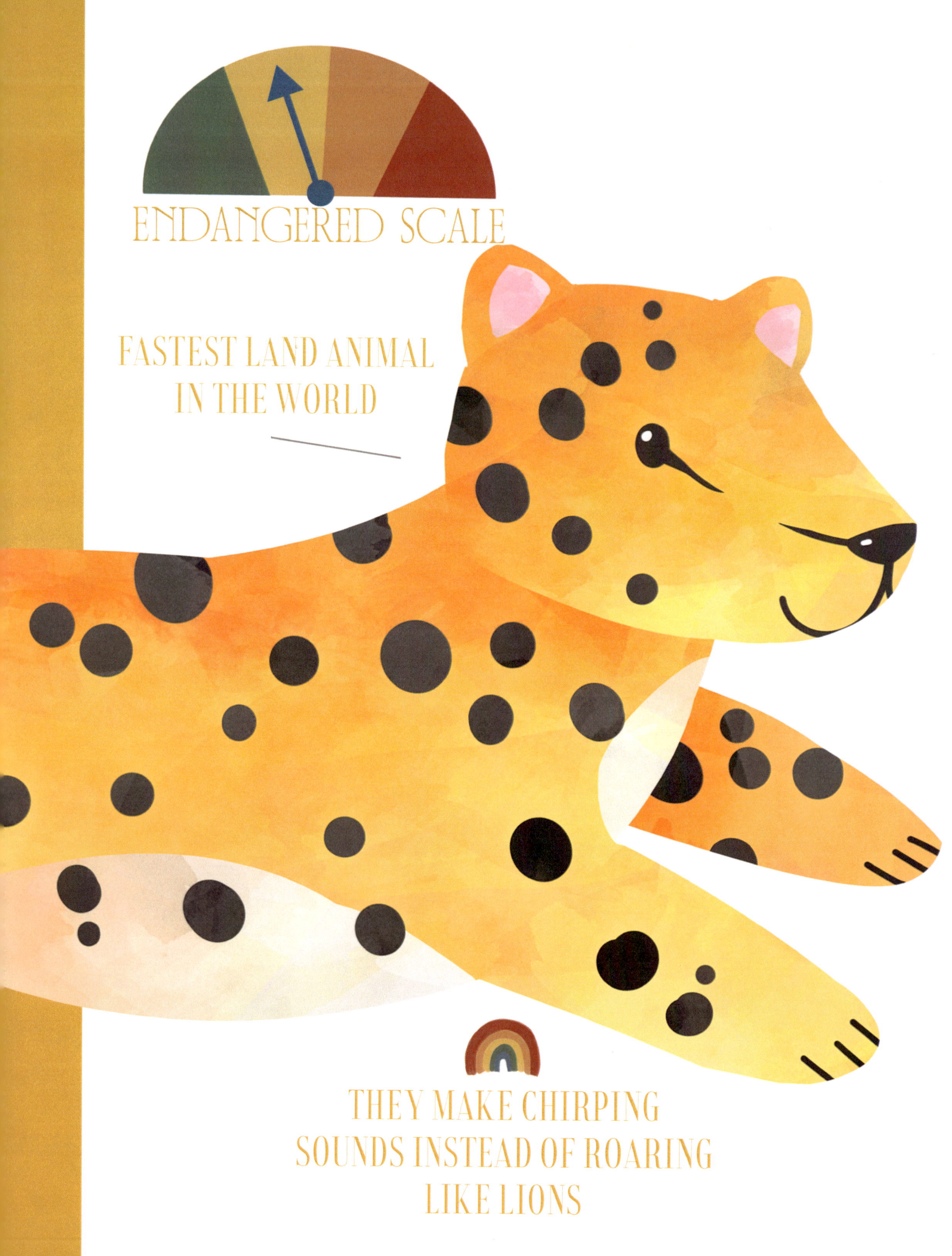
ENDANGERED SCALE
FASTEST LAND ANIMAL IN THE WORLD
THEY MAKE CHIRPING SOUNDS INSTEAD OF ROARING LIKE LIONS

CHEETAH

-MAMMAL-

LENGTH : 7 FEET

WEIGHT : 50 - 175 POUNDS

LIFESPAN : 15 - 20 YEARS

LOCATED : AFRICA

DIET : RABBITS, JACKALS,
SMALL ANTELOPE, AND GAZELLES

CLOUDLESS SULPHUR

-INSECT-

LENGTH : 2 - 3 INCHES

WEIGHT : UNKNOWN

LIFESPAN : 2 WEEKS

LOCATED : SOUTHERN
NORTH AMERICA

DIET : NECTAR

ONLY FEMALES
HAVE THE SMALL DOT
ON THE FOREWINGS
THEY HAVE REALLY LONG
TONGUES THAT CAN
REACH DEEP INTO FLOWERS
OTHER BUTTERFLIES CANNOT
ENDANGERED SCALE

DEATHSTALKER SCORPION

-ARACHNID-

LENGTH : 4 INCHES

WEIGHT : 1 GRAMS

LIFESPAN : 4 - 25 YEARS

LOCATED : NORTH AFRICA

DIET : INSECTS AND
OTHER INVERTEBRATES

ONLY THE STINGER HAS POISON FOR PREY
DESPITE THEIR SIZE THEY ARE THE MOST DANGEROUS SCORPION ON EARTH
ENDANGERED SCALE
?

EASTERN SAND DARTER

-BONY FISH-

LENGTH : 2 1/2 INCHES

WEIGHT : 1/2 - 2 GRAMS

LIFESPAN : 2 - 3 YEARS

LOCATED : EASTERN
NORTH AMERICA

DIET : INSECTS AND LARVAE

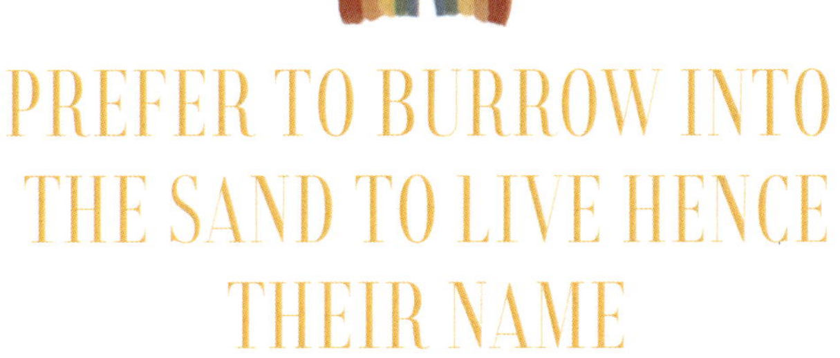

PREFER TO BURROW INTO
THE SAND TO LIVE HENCE
THEIR NAME

COLOR ALLOWS IT TO
CAMOUFLAGE IN THE SAND

EASTERN TIGER SWALLOWTAIL

-INSECT-

LENGTH : 6 INCHES

WEIGHT : 300 – 600 MILLIGRAMS

LIFESPAN : 3 WEEKS

LOCATED : NORTH AMERICA

DIET : NECTAR AND LEAVES

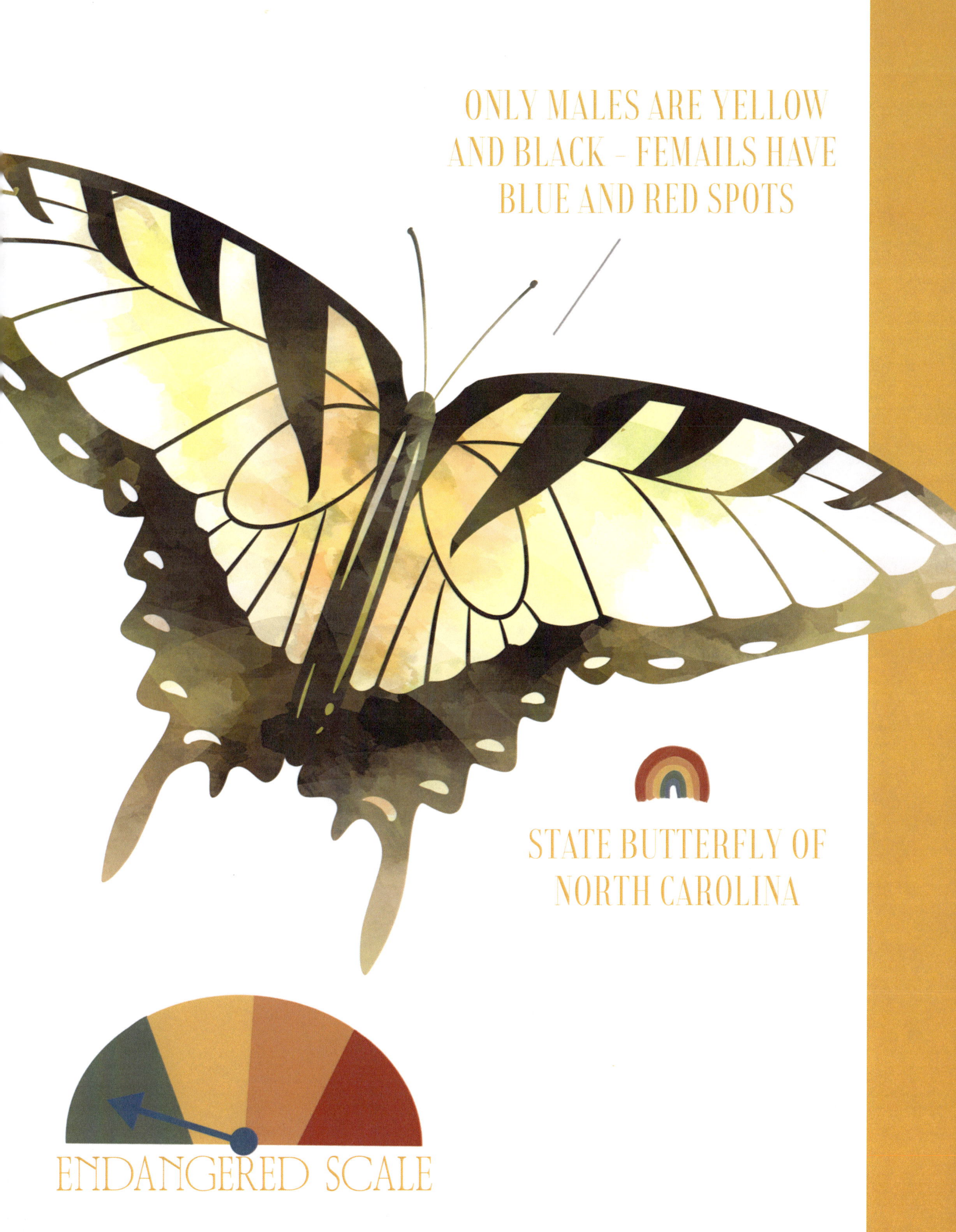

ONLY MALES ARE YELLOW AND BLACK – FEMAILS HAVE BLUE AND RED SPOTS
STATE BUTTERFLY OF NORTH CAROLINA
ENDANGERED SCALE

FISH WILL OFTEN
HIDE IN THEIR
TENTACLES
FROM PREDATORS
LARGEST JELLYFISH
IN THE OCEAN
ENDANGERED SCALE

LION'S MANE JELLYFISH

-CNIDARIAN-

LENGTH : 100 – 200 FEET

WEIGHT : 200 – 500 POUNDS

LIFESPAN : 1 YEAR

LOCATED : ARTIC AND NORTH PACIFIC OCEAN

DIET : ZOOPLANKTON, SMALL FISH, SHRIMP, AND OTHER JELLYFISH

LONG-SNOUTED SEAHORSE

-BONY FISH-

LENGTH : 10 INCHES

WEIGHT : 7 OUNCES - 1 POUND

LIFESPAN : 1 - 4 YEARS

LOCATED : ATLANTIC OCEAN
AND MEDITERRANEAN SEA

DIET : ZOOPLANKTON, SHRIMP,
SMALL FISH, AND PLANTS

THEY HAVE NO SCALES
LIKE OTHER BONY FISH

CAN CHANGE THEIR COLOR
TO BLACK, YELLOW, RED,
ORANGE, OR BROWN

ENDANGERED SCALE

VICEROY

-INSECT-

LENGTH : 2 - 3 INCHES

WEIGHT : 650 MILLIGRAMS

LIFESPAN : 2 WEEKS

LOCATED : SOUTHERN
NORTH AMERICA

DIET : NECTAR

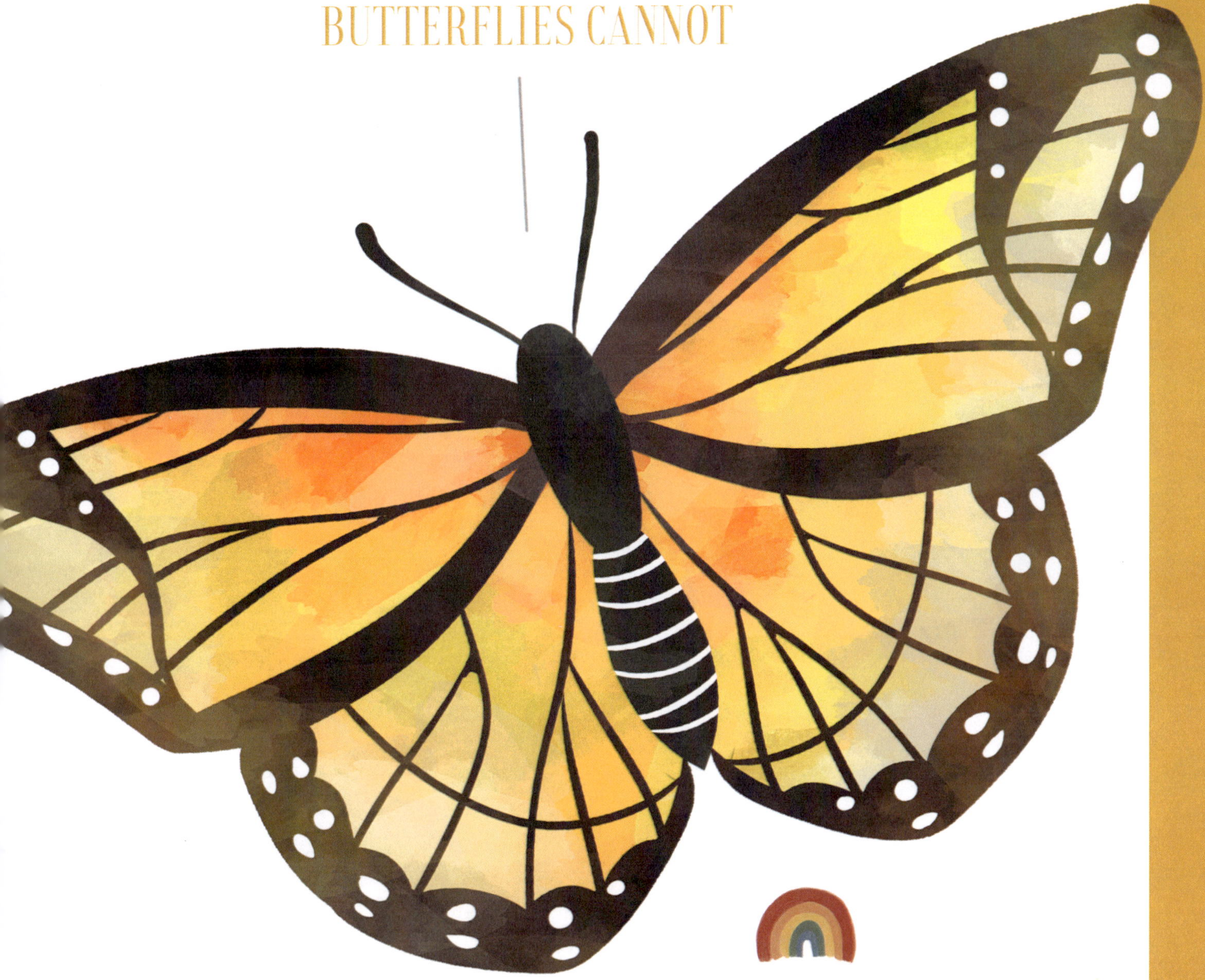

SIMILAR MARKINGS TO
MONARCH BUTTERFILES
TO MAKE PREDATORS
BELIEVE THEY ARE
POISONOUS AS WELL

YELLOW PERCH

-BONY FISH-

LENGTH : 10 – 12 INCHES

WEIGHT : 1/2 – 1 1/2 POUNDS

LIFESPAN : 10 – 11 YEARS

LOCATED : NORTH AMERICA

DIET : INSECTS, INVERTEBRATES
AND SMALLER FISH

DORSAL FIN IS MADE UP OF TWO PARTS WITH A SPACE IN BETWEEN
HAS MANY NICKNAMES SUCH AS "RACOON PERCH" AND "STRIPIES"
ENDANGERED SCALE

CATHLEEN AND LUCAS ARE A MOTHER - SON WRITING DUO.

CATHLEEN IS THE OWNER AND FOUNDER OF LDR PUBLISHING COMPANY.
SHE HAS BEEN WRITING AND ILLUSTRATING CHILDREN'S BOOKS
FOR MANY YEARS. HER SON, LUCAS, IS AN AVID READER
AND HAS BEEN A HUGE INSPIRATION IN HER DESIRE TO CREATE
BRILLIANT BOOKS FOR CHILDREN OF ANY AGE TO ENJOY!

LUCAS HAS BEEN WRITING ANIMAL BOOKS SINCE HE WAS
TWELVE YEARS OLD. THIS IS HIS FIRST BOOK SERIES.
THE ENTIRE IDEA FOR THE SERIES STARTED FROM HIS LOVE
OF NATURE AND ANIMALS. HE HAS STUDIED ANIMALS
SINCE HE WAS TWO YEARS OLD. AFTER READING HUNDREDS
OF BOOKS AND DOING YEARS OF RESEARCH, HE DECIDED
TO SHARE HIS KNOWLEDGE AND LOVE OF ANIMALS
WITH OTHER CHILDREN EVERYWHERE.

FEEL FREE TO CHECK OUT MORE OF THEIR
BOOK CREATIONS AT
WWW.LDRPUBLISHINGCOMPANY.COM

LDR Publishing Company

CATHLEEN AND LUCAS

RED
ORANGE
YELLOW
GREEN
BLUE

MAGENTA
BROWN
GREY
BLACK &
AND
RAINBOW